THE LITTLE BOOK OF

YORKSHIRE HUMOUR

Dalesman

First published in Great Britain 2010 by Dalesman Publishing
an imprint of
Country Publications Ltd
The Water Mill, Broughton Hall
Skipton, North Yorkshire BD23 3AG

Reprinted 2013, 2015

ISBN 978-1-85568-276-4

Printed in China on behalf of Latitude Press Ltd.

Introduction

If it is true that there are more acres in Yorkshire than there are letters in the Bible, then it must also be true that there have been even more jokes, funny stories and anecdotes uttered by its inhabitants over the years. Yorkshire folk have always had a humorous comment for every situation, succinctly expressed in Yorkshire dialect. Enjoy this selection of the best, from the readers of *Dalesman*, the region's favourite magazine.

A teacher from north of the border was taking a class of Yorkshire schoolboys, and he offered a prize of £5 for the best answer to the question: "Who is the greatest man in history?"

"Robert the Bruce," said Tommy.

The teacher handed over the money without demur. "But what was your reason for the answer you gave?" the teacher asked.

Tommy replied: "Well, Ah knoa deep dahn i' me awn 'eart 'at Ah should 'ave said Freddie Trueman, but business is business."

Young Johnny was proudly telling his dad that he been chosen for the part of an elderly man, thirty years married, in the school play.

"Well," said his dad, "I'm reight disappointed."

"Whatever for?" asked the lad.

"Because I thowt that this year tha'd at least ha' landed a speaking part."

The teacher in a Swaledale school had been telling the children the parable of the lost sheep. She asked the children why the shepherd was so pleased and overjoyed to find this one sheep when he still had the remaining ninety-nine in his flock.

There was a dead silence for a few seconds, then one bright little fellow replied:

"Well, miss, 'appen it wor t' tup."

The man at the pet shop said it was a sheep dog."

7

A doctor in Huddersfield was asked to attend a baby, who wailed bitterly as soon as he set eyes on him. The mother said tactfully:

"Tha mun tak' no notice o' t' bairn, doctor. He wor once freetened by a man wi' a fahl face."

Two youngsters boarded a bus in Keighley. The bigger of the two asked for a 'thruppence-hawpenny coomback'.

"Tha wants a what?" asked the conductor.

"A thruppence-hawpenny coomback."

"I suppose tha wants t' same?" the conductor said to the smaller lad.

"Nooa," was the reply, "I want a tuppenny stop theer."

One lovely feature of Yorkshire life was the custom of children calling at auntie's house about teatime, for a good tea was usually assured. A boy following this custom found two other visitors were present. When time came 'to draw up to the table' the boy was invited to say grace.

"You know," said auntie, "like your mother does at home."

Each head was bowed and the grace came clearly to the little boy:

"For God's sake go easy on the butter — it's half-a-crown a pound."

The teacher was reading from the Scriptures.

"Blessed are they that mourn…" and then interjected: "What is to mourn, Christopher?"

Replied the little lad brightly: "Wednesday."

A boy and his family moved from Yorkshire to Kent. Albert, being naturally taciturn, refused to speak when he attended his new school despite the efforts of a host of teachers, psychologists, speech therapists and psychiatrists. Then one day, at school dinner, Albert spoke out:

"This Yorkshire puddin's terrible."

His headmaster was overjoyed, but puzzled. "Why have you not spoken before?" he asked him.

"Well," replied Albert, surprised, "up to now, t' Yorkshire puddin's been all reet."

"Poor George — he just can't relax."

The stand-in teacher at the remote Dales school was trying to instil a little arithmetic into her class of five year olds. She pointed out of the window and enquired:

"How many sheep can you count in that field?"

There was a long pause.

"Well? ... Billy, do you know?"

Billy looked up at the teacher with an air of pitying superiority and replied:

"Them's noan sheep, miss. Them's tups."

A small boy, living near Sutton-in-Craven, was sent by his mother early one morning to a neighbouring farm, to borrow something.

Seeing the farmer milking in the cowshed, he enquired: "Is thi missus in?"

"She's in bed," the farmer replied, "and thee don't go disturbin' 'er. T' first thing she'll do will be to put t' leet on, then she'll come dahnstairs and leet a fire. Next she'll put t' kettle on and make hersen some teea, then she'll want summat to eeat. Let 'er alone, she's costing nowt theer."

A visitor to Scarborough fell into conversation with one of the old fishermen in the harbour. The fisherman was saying how his family line had been traced back to the Norman Conquest, and they had always been in the fishing industry. The visitor then jokingly remarked:

"I suppose if you go back far enough, you would find that one of your ancestors sailed with Noah in the Ark."

"I don't think so," replied the fisherman. "You see, we've always had our own boat."

A group of anglers were relating their experiences in the bar of a Wharfedale inn.

"I was once fishing on a Scottish loch," boasted one, "and caught one so big that the others wouldn't let me haul it into the boat in case it swamped us."

"Oh aye," said the old dalesman sitting at the corner of the bar. "Same thing 'appened to me once — when I were on t' *Queen Elizabeth*."

"Has anyone handed in a boat?"

Having reached the age of sixty, Joe, a Huddersfield weaver, was no longer able to do his regular job, and his wife was greatly distressed at this state of affairs. Then one day he came home and said:

"Buck up, lass, Ah've getten a job as a neet watchman."

His wife burst into tears.

"Well, if that isn't t' limit," she said, sobbing, "just when Ah've made thee two new neet-shirts."

Two old farmworkers were chatting at the bar of a quiet village pub on the North York Moors, when in walked a well-dressed young couple.

"What will you have, dahling?" the young man asked his companion.

"Gin and tonic, dear," she replied.

One old farmworker turned to the other and whispered, "Them's nut married."

When asked how he knew, he said: "If they 'ad been, he would've just bought her half a shandy wi'out asking, and there'd be no 'darling'."

Stan wandered slowly home from a visit to the doctor's surgery with the verdict of his consultation sitting heavily on his mind. On reaching home he found his wife busy working upstairs. Going to the foot of the stairs he called out:

"Eeh, Norma lass, I'm bahn to 'ave t' appendicitis!"

Quickly the retort came from above:

"Tha's heving nowt till Ah've 'ed a new 'at!"

"Stop saying 'It could have been worse'."

An old Yorkshireman was lying ill in bed, approaching the end. His wife and the doctor stood at the end of the bed.

Said the doctor to the wife: "I don't think he's got long to go now."

The man's voice was heard faintly from the bed: "Nay, I don't feel so bad today."

"Hod thi din!" exclaimed his wife. "T' doctor knaws better than thee."

A junior reporter in Batley called at a house in the town to get the particulars of a man who had died. The widow was very friendly, and asked if he would like to see the body. Unable to refuse, the reporter did so, and expressed the view that the deceased looked very peaceful. The widow examined the body closely and then remarked:

"Aye, he does an' all, doesn't he? But then he were always a bit slow on the uptake, were Albert, so happen he hasn't realised what's happened to him yet."

Two lads, Jack and Bill, were brought up in the same village and were close pals all their schooldays. Afterwards they had to go out to earn their living, and they drifted apart. It was many years before they met again. At last they met, and Jack says to Bill:

"Hello, Bill, how's ta going on? Ah hear thou's married. What's t' wife like?"

"Oh," says Bill, "she's a little angel. What's thine like?"

"Nay," says Jack, "mine isn't deead yet."

A retired couple from upper Calderdale had been shopping in Halifax. They were boarding the one and only bus back to their village when the conductor informed the old man that there was only room for one more person.

Without further ado, the old man climbed aboard the bus and, turning to his wife, who was behind him, said to her:

"Ah'll have a cup o' tea waiting for thee when tha gets home."

Overheard at a WI meeting in York:

"And how is your husband getting on?"

"I hardly know. He is so very very busy, I only see him for about an hour a day."

"Oh, you poor thing. I am sorry."

"Oh, that's all right. The hour soon passes."

A miner who had overslept was hurriedly getting dressed for his day shift.

"Alf," said his wife in a voice like a whiplash. "Tha's putting thi clogs on t' wrong feet."

"Ah know," said he. "They ought to be on thine."

A group of pals were chatting in
the pub one evening when one of
them joked that another in their
group was hen-pecked.

"Mebbe so," he replied, "but it's
grand bein' pecked bi reight 'en."

On the spur of the moment, Ned had gone away one Friday for a weekend's sea-fishing at Scarborough with his pals, but now it was Sunday evening and they were all sat in the pub ready to go home.

"Doesn't t' Owd Book say that Jonah wor in a whale's belly for three days?" asked Ned.

"What's that to do wi' thee?" replied one of his pals.

"Nay," sighed Ned, "Ah were just wondering if 'is wife believed 'im when 'e got home an' told 'er where 'e'd been."

"Did you 'ear that owd Dick Smith's gettin' wed agin?"

"You'd 'ave thowt he were owd enough to know better nor that."

"Aye, he does know better, lad — but trouble is, he met a widder who knew better still."

A farmer one night saw a light moving across the farmyard, and discovered it was being carried by his farmhand. On being asked where he was going with the light, the farmhand replied: "Ah'm off courtin'."

"Courtin'?" queried the farmer. "Ah nivver took a lantern when Ah went courtin'."

"Naw," replied the farmhand, "Ah thowt not when Ah saw thi missus."

A Grassington man, celebrating his marriage, was making his speech at the wedding breakfast:

"Ah reckon my new missus is exactly reight. If she'd been any better, Ah shouldn't hev got 'er. If she'd been any worse, Ah wouldn't hev hed 'er. So Ah reckon she's exactly reight."

"It's her fifth wedding."

A Yorkshire gamekeeper was discussing a day's shoot and also his difficulty in finding the proper title for one of his guests, a bishop.

"I noar reet well that a lord or a herl I calls 'im 'Lord', and a dook 'Yer Grace', but t' bishop fair bested me. I were standin' near 'im, and up jumps a rabbit. I shouts out 'Shoot the little b----r, Yer 'Oliness!', but I could see by t' expression on 'is face I war wrong."

A rambler, out one spring morning on a Pennine summit, met an old farmer mending a drystone wall. It was a glorious day; the hills shone, green near at hand, blue in the distance. The rambler nodded to the farmer and said: "Fine morning."

The farmer gave him a glance of scorn and replied witheringly:

"Well, dooan't let's get into a lather abaht it."

"Shep likes to get them into the pen in his own way."

An old and somewhat irascible farmer working on the moors near Helmsley was having great difficulty in getting his sheepdog to drive the flock from one field into another. In desperation, and truly vexed, he shouted:

"Thoo useless b----r! Coom 'ere an' 'old gate oppen an Ah'll drive 'em through mesen."

A Dales farmer had to undergo a rather serious operation, performed privately by an eminent Leeds surgeon. In due course the question of payment arose.

"The bill is fifty guineas," said the surgeon.

The farmer proceeded to count out a pile of £1 notes very slowly.

"Oh, give me a cheque," said the surgeon, "and save yourself a lot of trouble."

"Nay, nay," replied the farmer, "Ah've put thee down in my income tax returns as ten tons o' muck."

When an old Wolds farmer was told by his doctor to change to a healthier and simpler diet, he objected most strongly:

"Aw'm nut gooing to starve mysen to death for t' sake o' living a few years longer."

A Calderdale farmer was stood on the hillside, moodily regarding the ravaging effects of a flood.

"Kit," called a neighbour, "Ah've just seen all your sheep washed down the river."

"What about Robinson's sheep?" asked the farmer.

"Oh, they've gone."

"And Calvert's?"

"Oh aye, they've gone too."

"Ah well," said the farmer, cheering up. "Maybe it isn't as bad as Ah thowt."

In Bradford lived two brothers, in business as coal dealers, and their reputation for honest dealing was not of the highest. One of the brothers started to attend church, became 'converted' and then set about to reform his kith and kin. In the end it came to a showdown. The other brother, quite exasperated, retorted thus:

"Nah look here, it's all vary well for thee to talk, but Ah'm baan to ask thi a straight question: If Ah get converted, who does ta think's baan to weight t' coil?"

A young and keen accountant was assisting a not-so-young and world-weary Dales farmer with the work of filling out a very long and very detailed application form to register the farm as a business for VAT. The accountant read out question after question, and the farmer answered them all.

Finally the accountant asked: "Will your records be kept on a computer?"

To which the farmer replied: My records'll be kept on t' same bl--dy spike they've allus been kept on!"

"No I don't want a filing cabinet as a Christmas present — what I want is an incinerator."

A visitor from London was watching the blacksmith in Helmsley making a wrought-iron gate. The visitor finally commented:

"It's nice to see a true craftsman at work. I work in the small instrument field where I've got to be accurate to 1/10,000th of an inch."

The blacksmith looked up at him and replied:

"Weel, in that case, thoo'd better stay an' watch. Ah's exact."

A villager asked about the proficiency of the local joiner, as he wanted to buy a wheelbarrow.

"Aye," explained a local, "thee can go and ask 'im to do t' job, an' if thy wheelbarrow runs as well as 'is watter-butts, it'll be a good un."

"Ploughman's lunch, please."

Farmer George was asked how his son, who was at agricultural college, was coming along with his studies.

"Well, tha knows," replied Farmer George, "he still ploughs t' same way, but he talks different. He allus used to say 'Whoa, Ned' when he gat to th' end o' t' furrow, and then it was 'Gee up, lad'. Now he's that posh he says, 'Halt, Edward; pivot and proceed.' T' horse can't understand him. So I'm telling you, it's no good sending anybody away to learn farming unless tha sends t' horse an' all."

The mayor of a certain West Riding town, who had had a very busy year, became ill. The town council met and proposed that the alderman should visit the mayor's house and express the sympathy of the council. The alderman said to the mayor:

"Last night it was proposed that I come round and express the council's sympathy and the hope that you soon recover, and the motion was passed — by eight votes to seven."

Tom, on entering the mill canteen, was greeted with:

"Noo, lad, 'ow's tha gettin' on?"

"Oh, nut sa bad, but Ah's a lartle bit tired."

"That isn't wi' wark, 'cos thu disn't like it all that mitch, does tha?"

"Nay, mebbe nut. But thoo naws, a cat likes milk, but thoo nivver knew yan droon itsen amang it, did tha?"

"There's a weed in yon field."

An old farmer near Masham was asked in the village pub how his hens were laying.

"They've all stopped, every one of them," he replied.

"Can you account for it?" asked the landlord.

"I believe I can," the farmer said. "It's like this. I've been having a shippon built and the bricklayers have been on piece-work. I'll swear my hens were listening when them chaps were swanking about the wages they earn laying bricks."

A Yorkshire farmer, visiting a café in Hawes on market day, was asked if he would like some trifle. He replied:

"Na, na. Ah wean't hev onny o' that — thur's ovver monny teastes at yance i' that."

A butcher's lad was riding his carrier bicycle very fast down Pateley Bridge High Street — too fast, in fact. He suddenly toppled over and crashed, sprawling over his bike and sending the contents of its basket everywhere. Passers-by gave assistance. On being asked if he was all right, the lad replied:

"Ah'm alreight — but Ah've lost me heart, me liver's mucky, and one of me kidneys has rolled down that drain."

"Hey, mam! Can this camper have a bucket o' watter?"

An elderly farmer had been having treatment for his rheumatics, which was very effective. A friend said to him:

"Well, Ah reckon tha's fair set up wi' theesen noo thee's getten rid o' t' rheumatics."

"Nay, Ah doan't know so much," was the reply. "Tha see's, Ah carn't tell noo when it's gahn ti rain."

"Today: gave up smoking."

In a doctor's surgery somewhere near Rotherham, the doctor was speaking to a patient.

"Do you know you've been going about with a broken arm? Why didn't you come to me before?"

"Well," was the patient's reply, "every time Ah says something is wrang wi' me, t' wife maks me stop smoking."

Old Sam was badly out of sorts, so his family sent for the doctor.

"My good man," the doctor said. "Unless you give up drinking at once, you will be blind."

Old Sam pondered a while and then replied:

"Ah'm gettin old. Ah've been to St Leger at Doncaster, Ah've seen York Minster, and Ah've visited Bridlington. There's nowt much left to see. Ah'll risk it."

"Keep off the caviar, asparagus tips and champagne."

63

The cricket team from a South Yorkshire mining village was playing an away match in the neighbouring village. In the first four balls, 'their' umpire disallowed three plum LBW appeals by the opening fast bowler, who was also the captain.

Returning to the start of his run-up and then hitching up his trousers for the task ahead, he bellowed out in a voice loud enough to be heard back in his own village:

"Reyt, lads, we'll get nowt 'ere — we'll just 'ave to bowl this lot out."

A rugby league match was taking place between two West Yorkshire teams who were the fiercest of rivals. The hard-fought match had reached a critical stage, with the score tied at 18-18. Several players had already been carried off injured, and several more had their jerseys ripped, when a particularly strong kick by one of the full-backs sent the ball right out of the ground. The players hesitated, wondering what to do next, when a voice from the crowd shouted:

"Nivver mind t' ball, lads, just gerron wi' t' game!"

The Nonconformist chapel was badly in need of repair, and the minister told the congregation that it would cost at least £5,000. Immediately a wealthy but stingy member of the congregation said that he would contribute £5 to the effort. Just as he sat down, a lump of plaster fell from the ceiling and hit him on the head, whereupon he hastily said that he had made a mistake and would in fact like to contribute £50.

This was all too much for the minister, who called out: "Hallelujah! Hit him again, Lord, hit him again!"

A Yorkshire moorland parson, visiting his flock, called upon an old farmer who rarely went to church. He was gratified to find him poring intently over his Bible, while three pups gambolled at his feet.

"Well, well, John," said the parson. "It is indeed a pleasure to see you mending the error of your ways in your old age."

"Nowt o' t' sooart, vicar," was the reply. "To tell yer t' truth, Ah'm lookin' for names for t' pups."

The weather was very cold, and the organist of a small Yorkshire church reprimanded the caretaker (who was also the organ blower) for not having the church sufficiently heated.

"It's almost too cold for me to play the organ," he grumbled.

After the service, the caretaker was overheard laughing and saying:

"He's allus hevving a go at me, but I got me revenge toneet. When he were playing *Christians Awake*, I were blowing for *God Rest Ye Merry Gentlemen*."

"What do you mean, you feel wicked?"

A farmer at Horton-in-Ribblesdale had a horse and trap. One day he gave the local vicar a lift from one end of the village to the vicarage.

But instead of stopping at the vicarage, the horse went on for some considerable distance, without the driver attempting to arrest it. The vicar mentioned this to the old farmer, who replied:

"Aye, I know, but she'll nut stop unless I give a good cussing and I didn't like to when thou was there."

Two Yorkshiremen had had rather too much to drink. As they stumbled along a country road, they had a heated argument about what they saw in the heavens. One asserted it was the sun. The other was equally certain it was the moon. Seeing another man approaching, they appealed to him.

"Mister, isn't that t' sun?" said one.

The other chimed in: "Nay, it's mooin, isn't it?"

Not wishing to be involved, he replied: "Well, to tell yer t' truth, Ah'm a stranger i' theeas parts."

"You'd look green if you'd come from Mars to Heckmondwike in half an hour."

73

Overheard at the York Mystery Plays: two Americans were watching one of the plays performed in broad Yorkshire dialect, and one remarked:

"Oh, George, they talk just like they do in *Dalesman*."

The pronunciation of the word 'bath' has always been a source of dispute between North and South.

A young man from the South, now resident in Yorkshire, was asked what he called it. He wasn't sure.

"You see," he explained, "the people I'm living with have got me into the way of calling it a 'wash-all-over'."

A little lad was being taken for a bus ride in the Dales by his mother. The bus crossed a bridge over the River Wharfe.

"Look, mam," he exclaimed, "there's a waterfall."

"Weir, dear," gently reproved his mother.

"Theer," the little lad replied.

Two small boys stood looking up at the statue of Sir Titus Salt in Manningham Park. One of them read out the title inscribed underneath: "Sir Titus Salt, Bart."

Turning to the other one he said: "What does 'Bart' mean?"

The other one looked up at the statue again and replied:

"Why, baht 'at, of course."

A French girl had married a British soldier at the end of the First World War, and came to settle with him in a small town in Yorkshire. She always retained a strong French accent but acquired a considerable grasp of the local idiom.

To earn extra money she took on the job of cleaning the church hall, with satisfactory results. She told a neighbour:

"Ze church 'all is far bettair now. Before it vos, 'ow you say, mucky as owt."

Many years ago, a Yorkshire lady rang her coal merchant to order a supply of coal and asked for an early delivery, adding "S'il vous plaît".

The coal merchant asked her what she meant by this. She explained that, as we had just joined the Common Market, we must practise our French and she was trying it out.

"Oh, in that case madam," said the merchant, "how would you like it — cul de sac or à la carte?"

"*Just three more miles and we should be
in sight of Malham Tarn…*"

A fellwalker entered a Dales inn and got into conversation with a local farmer.

"Will you have another one?" asked the walker, after several glasses of ale had been drunk.

"Nay," was the reply. "Ah munnat stop. Ah've t' van outside wi' t' lambs, sheep and t' missus in it."

Two locals were discussing a mutual friend who had lost much weight.

"He's that thin now," said one, "he's like a ha'porth o' sooap after a lang day's wesh."

Tom the village postman was so dedicated to his job that he hadn't taken a holiday in over thirty years. His work colleagues told him he ought to get away for a week, and suggested Bridlington. At last Tom reluctantly agreed, and a relief postman took over his round. The next week Tom was back at work.

"By, Tom lad," a colleague remarked, "you look better for your week off; did you go to Brid?"

"Nay," replied Tom, "it were such a grand week, Ah've bin going round with t' relief postman."

In Leeds magistrates' court, a loquacious witness was told by the presiding magistrate to be a little more terse in his evidence.

"I suppose you know what terse means?" asked the magistrate.

'Course I do — it's t' first coach at a funeral."

Old Enoch lived in a Dales village with his ailing wife. He was usually to be found sitting near the cottage door making odds and ends out of timber he found round about the village.

One day, when the doctor called, Enoch was sitting outside hammering nails into some pieces of wood.

"How is your wife today?" asked the doctor.

"Oh pretty bad, sir, pretty bad."

"Is that her coughing?"

"Oh no," said Enoch, "this is a chicken coop."

In the 1930s an urban district council in South Yorkshire had completed its first council housing estate, and the housing committee sat in solemn conclave, trying to find a name for it.

"That's easy," said one of the members. "Ah reckon that we owt ter cal 'em T' Cloisters."

"Cloisters?" exclaimed the others, mystified.

"Aye, because they're clois ter t' shops, they're clois ter t' pub, they're clois ter t' cinema, they're clois ter t' church, they're clois ter t' cemetry. They're clois ter ivverything."

A Southern woman became a teacher at a school near Bradford. On the first day she accumulated a quantity of rubbish and left her classroom in search of the dustbin. One of the other teachers was returning from the direction of the school gate.

"Where's the bin?" she enquired.

"Ah've bin t' Black Bull, if it's owt to do wi' thee," came the blunt reply.

Freda and Joe decided to go to a 'posh' place for lunch. The soup arrived, very hot, and Joe started blowing it noisily.

"Nay Joah, tha doesn't do that in posh spots lahke this."

"Wat mun I do then? It's too hot to sup."

"Tha mun waft it with thi cap."

"When I was little we had a dog called Grieg, after t' composer, like."

"That's odd. Did it like classical music or summat?"

"No, it used to pee agin t' suite."

"I figured they'd be more scared of my wife."

A Wolds farmer devised a marvellous scarecrow. It waved its arms in the breeze. It had an alarming tin rattle that went off at intervals. And it carried a dummy gun. He was asked if it really scared the birds after all his effort.

"Noo, Ah reckons it does. Whya, only the other day they crows brought back some corn they had stole from me two years ago."

A Barnsley man was so fond of his Yorkshire terrier that when it died he took it to a taxidermist and asked him to stuff and then gold-plate his pet as a permanent memorial.

"Eighteen carats?" asked the taxidermist.

"No," the man replied, "chewing a bone."

Two youngsters were sitting in the kitchen playing 'I Spy'.

Billy (a true Yorkshireman) said 'T'; and Tommy (from Essex), after guessing 'Table', 'Teaspoon', 'Tea towel' etc, gave up.

Triumphantly, Billy said:

"T' oven door."

The junior school class, in a small village at the foot of the Pennines, was studying spelling. The teacher was explaining how the letter Q is always followed by the letter U. Examples were flowing freely, and the word 'quoit' was given.

"Anyone not know what a quoit is?" asked the teacher.

The class looked mystified.

"Michael," said the teacher, "go and fetch me a quoit."

Off went Michael, proud and pleased to be chosen, and returned triumphantly — with his overcoat.

Jimmy, from Yorkshire, was being introduced to Ben, from Lancashire.

"Tha's from Yorkshire, eh?" asked Ben.

"Aye, lad," replied Jimmy.

"Well give us thi other hand as well — last Yorkshireman Ah shook hands with, picked me pocket."

Tom was born this side of Oldham, at Springhead; and that makes him a Yorkshireman. But his twang at the time could have misled anybody into thinking he was a 'Lanky'. When he moved to a Midlands town, his twang was noticed by Lancastrians there and he was asked to join their society.

"But I'm a Yorkshireman," he protested.

"It doesn't matter," came the reply. "You talk like one of us. Besides, t' treasurer's job's open and we've nobody we can trust wi' t' brass."

In the refreshment room of the old Midland Station in Leeds, a middle-aged lady was struggling with a hot cup of tea, trying to gulp it down before her train departed and also keeping an eye on the clock as she did so.

An old man nearby saw her plight and called out:

"'Ere, missus, tak my cup o' tea — it's already saucered and blowed."

A musical concert was to be held at Runswick Bay, and organising it had been left to a somewhat unmusical lady. She drew up a list of all the different sections of the concert such as 'choir', 'duet', 'solo', etc.

However, when the chairman read through the programme he suddenly noticed one item headed 'O-O-O'. He asked the lady organiser what 'O-O-O' was supposed to mean.

The lady turned round and indignantly replied:

"Don't be daft, man, that means trio!"

In the 1930s there was an amateur concert party which used to perform at church socials and the like. One winter Sunday evening they arrived at a church hall near Doncaster and were met by the verger.

"Theer's t' dressin' room," he said, indicating a small vestry.

"Dressing room?" queried the concert party secretary. "But there are ladies and gentlemen in the party."

"Well," replied the old man belligerently. "What's t' matter? 'Ave they 'ad words or summat?"

A leader of the amateur operatic society which was performing at Batley Town Hall, on being asked how *Goodnight Vienna* was going down in Batley, replied:

"Oh, about as well as *Goodnight Batley* would go down in Vienna."

"Somebody has cut the appendix out of this book."

A rather shy girl entered the mobile library while it was parked in Leyburn, and then paused as if lost.

"What book would you like?" asked the librarian in charge.

"Where do you keep 'Romance?'," asked the girl.

Explained the librarian helpfully: "You'll find 'Romance' in that dark little corner over there, miss."

And a very embarrassed male borrower already in that dark little corner moved away quickly.

A very well-known watercolour artist was painting next to a village pub in Dentdale. Presently, up came a village elder, who looked at the work, then said:

"By gum, lad, that's all reight. I'll tell thee what: when tha's done it, tha wants to tak it into t' pub, tha'll get a fiver for it, 'cos Ah've sin 'em give a fiver for a lot worse na that."

An artist was painting at Bolton Castle when a local farmer stopped to talk and view the work in progress. They conversed for some time. Then there was a short silence. Said the farmer:

"Tell me, is it reight you fellers nivver 'ave owt till after yer dee?"

"You keep saying 'Don't cross your bridges until you come to them'. Well, we've come to them."

A Halifax man, troubled by his wife's reckless way with money, finally gave her an account book and £100 for the housekeeping.

"Now," he said. "Thoo put down what Ah've gi'en thoo on one page, and on t' opposite page put down what thoo's done wi' it. Then thoo'll know wheer all t' money's gone."

At the end of the week she handed the book to her husband. "Look, I've done just as you told me."

And she had. On one page was written: '£100 received'. On the opposite page was written: 'Spent it'.

A preacher in Bridlington, on the first Sunday after the declaration of war in 1939, prayed earnestly:

"Oh Lord, as Thou wilt 'ave seen i' yesterday's *Yorkshire Post*, them Germans is at it agen."

During the last war a German plane was shot down, crash-landing in a field near a village in Holderness. The shocked and bleeding pilot crawled out of the wreckage, to be confronted by a grim-looking Yorkshire farmhand. The German indicated that he was wounded, looking for sympathy.

The response was pointed and brief. The farmhand replied, in broad East Riding dialect:

"Well! Tho shun't 'a' cum!"

"Look here, my man," said the lady in a Harrogate suburb, "will you please inform me why you come begging for food at my door again and again? Why don't you try some of the other people in the road?"

"I can't," replied the tramp. "It's doctor's orders, mum."

"Doctor's orders?"

"Yes, mum. My doctor told me that when I found the food that agreed with me I should continue with it."

"On a cold morning you should always warm your hands."

A Richmond couple had moved to a more rural area of Swaledale. The wife had felt obliged to reprimand the new milkman whose deliveries were apt to be haphazard.

One morning she opened the door and found a milkless doorstep plus a cow grazing placidly in the back garden. Despondently she remarked to her husband:

"Ah'm afeared yon milkman's taken t' huff. He's left us a do-it-yoursen kit."

"You can't frighten them with Hell Fire — they're used to central heating."

A vicar in the parsonage of a remote parish in the North York Moors heard strange noises one night and, getting out of bed to investigate, found a man creeping about the living room.

"What are you seeking, lad?" asked the vicar.

The intruder said "Money".

"Half a minute," said the vicar, "I'll get a candle and help you."

The vicar was inspecting a class of Dales schoolchildren on their knowledge of the Scriptures.

"What does it mean where we read of Our Lord, 'And they were astonished at His Doctrine'?" he asked.

Up went one little boy's hand.

"Please sir," he said. "They were fair capped."

In an East Riding village pub some years ago, an old chap walked in with a bag of empty beer bottles and dumped them on the bar.

"Them dead uns?" inquired the landlord.

"Aye," said the old chap, "and Ah wor wi 'em when they were dying."

"That tractor thoo selled me's a bad 'un. Will tha tak it back?"

"Not likely; thoo should ha' found out afore tho bought it."

"Then I'll tak tha ti court."

"Please thissen but thoo knows what t' judge'll say."

"What?"

"He'll say, 'Caveat emptor'."

"And what does that mean?"

"It means thoo's had it."

While visiting his son in London, a Dales farmer noticed four road labourers taking a breather, leaning on their shovels.

"Typical Southerners," the farmer growled. "Three doin' nowt an' one helpin' 'em."

An old farmer had never been to York although he always wanted to see the city, so he went for the day and had a pleasant few hours looking round. Then he went to a restaurant for a meal. He began with chicken soup.

He looked puzzled when he tasted it. "What do they call this?" he asked.

"Chicken soup," the waiter replied.

"Nay," he commented. "That chicken must 'ave walked through this soup on stilts."

"I hear tell that t' flu epidemic's ovver i' most parts, but that we've not heard o' t' end of it, like."

"We shan't hear t' end on it at our house till t' bottle's empty."

"What bottle?"

"Well, tha sees, ivver sin' Fred found we'd a bottle o' whisky left ovver from Christmas, he's been doin' nowt but ward off t' symptoms."

The vicar of Staincliffe had the degree of MA. He kept a small herd of cows on the glebe-land, employing a youth to do the milking and distribute the milk. This was done from a pony cart which had the vicar's name painted on the side. When someone asked about the meaning of the letters 'MA', the youth would reply:

"They mean Milk 'Awker."

Sheffield man to his pal in the Lake District:

"There's nowt here but scenery."

On a coach tour of Wales, the driver stopped the coach as it skirted the base of Snowdon. He waxed very poetically, pointing upwards:

"Look you, people, is it not a wonderful sight?"

A sceptical Yorkshireman said grudgingly:

"Aye, but when all's said an' done, lad, it's nowt but a gert big lump o' muck."

In a Skipton back street the talk was between two five-year-old girls:

"Sylvia, have you got that chewing gum that I lent you?"

"No, I've lost it."

"Well, you'll have to find it, 'cos it's our Robert's."

A note found in a book in Keighley
Library:

"Joe, when you've read up to here,
please take the pie out of the oven."

Other books published by Dalesman:

Yorkshire Humour
The Little Book of Yorkshire
The Little Book of Yorkshire Dialect
The Little Book of Yorkshire Proverbs
Yorkshire Dialect Classics
Yorkshire Dialect Dictionary

For a full list of our books, calendars,
DVDs, videos and magazines,
visit www.dalesman.co.uk

THE LITTLE BOOK OF
YORKSHIRE HUMOUR

Yorkshire folk have always been renowne
for their humorous, insightful and
down-to-earth outlook on life. The proof
is in this little book, crammed full of
Yorkshire jokes, sayings and anec
in traditional Yorkshire dialect, take
the pages of *Dalesman*, the coun
favourite magazine.

ISBN-13: 978-1855682764

9 781855 682764

£2.9

Dalesma

KS-253-542